Independence Day

Birthday of the United States

Elaine Landau

E

For Joshua Garmizo

Library of Congress Cataloging-in-Publication Data

Landau, Elaine.
Independence Day—birthday of the United States / Elaine Landau.
     p. cm. — (Finding out about holidays)
Includes bibliographical references (p.) and index.
ISBN 0-7660-1571-8 (alk. paper)
1. Fourth of July—Juvenile literature. 2. Fourth of July celebrations—Juvenile literature.
[1. Fourth of July. 2. Holidays.] I. Title. II. Series.
E286 .L27 2001
394.2634—dc21
     00-009425

Printed in the United States of America

10 9 8 7 6 5 4 3 2 1

To Our Readers:
All Internet Addresses in this book were active and appropriate when we went to press. Any comments or
suggestions can be sent by e-mail to Comments@enslow.com or to the address on the back cover.

Photo Credits: Archive Photos, pp. 4, 6, 7, 8, 9, 10 (both), 11, 12, 13, 15, 18, 22, 23, 24, 25 (both), 28, 31; Corel Corportion, pp. 1, 2, 3, 17, 26, 27, 30, 33 (both), 35, 39, 46, 47, 48; © Hemera Technologies Inc., 1997–2000, pp. 5, 44 (all), 45 (all); Jeff Greenburg/Archive Photos, p. 16; Lambert/Archive Photos, pp. 19, 29; Reuters/Brad Rickerby/ Archive Photos, p. 40; Reuters/Brendan McDermid/Archive Photos, p. 21; Reuters/ Cameron Craig/Archive Photos, p. 34; Reuters/Molly Riley/Archive Photos, pp. 38, 41; Reuters/Neal Lauron/Archive Photos, p. 20; Reuters/Stelios Varias/Archvie Photos, p. 36; Reuters/Tim Shaffer/Archive Photos, p. 37; Reuters/Win McNamee/Archive Photos, p. 32.

Cover Photos: Archive Photos (top); Lambert/Archive Photos (middle); Corel Corporation (bottom); Corel Corporation (background).

CONTENTS

People all over America celebrate the Fourth of July. Watching fireworks is a fun thing to do.

CHAPTER 1

Come and Celebrate

Fireworks! Picnics! Parades! Red, white, and blue streamers are everywhere. Hot dogs cook on the grill. Children wave small flags. People across America are celebrating. It must be July 4, Independence Day.

Everyone has a birthday, and so does America. The United States of America was born on July 4, 1776. Before that, the king of England ruled. On July 4, Americans declared their independence. The United States would become a new nation, with its own laws, leaders, and flag.

In 1776, people celebrated their independence from England. Today, Americans still remember their nation's birthday. Every July 4 they celebrate.

FOURTH OF JULY FUN

Fireworks are a fun and exciting way to help celebrate America's birthday. They help us to remember the fight that took place for our independence.

5

This painting shows the signing of the Declaration of Independence. The American colonies declared their freedom from England with this document.

CHAPTER 2

Let Freedom Ring

Every year on July 4 in the United States of America, we celebrate our independence. But the very first Independence Day was celebrated on July 8, 1776. Long ago, in the days before telephones and television, news traveled slowly by horseback or by ship. It took many days for copies of the Declaration of Independence to reach all thirteen American colonies.

In 1776, our country did not have fifty states. There were just thirteen colonies. These colonies were settlements that belonged to England. They were scattered along the East Coast of North America.

Most of the people in the American colonies were born in England. They came to the colonies hoping for a better life. Some hoped to find freedom in this new land. But many of the colonists did not think they had found that freedom.

King George III ruled England. He also ruled the American colonies. The king asked a lot of

Many people came to the American colonies hoping for a better life.

the colonists. England was a powerful country. It had many soldiers and weapons, and lots of armed ships. But it took a great deal of money for England to stay that powerful. The thirteen American colonies created businesses and farmed the land to make money for England.

England's soldiers protected the American colonies, so England's king felt that taxes should be paid to him for this protection. A tax is money from the sale of things such as molasses, sugar, stamps, or tea. The colonists believed they were not being taken care of by the king and did not want to pay the taxes. The king sent soldiers to the American colonies to make sure that the taxes were paid. The colonists had to provide places to stay and food for the soldiers.

The colonists decided the king of England was unfair, so they took action. In 1774, a leader from each of the American colonies met in Philadelphia, Pennsylvania. This meeting became known as the Continental Congress. The leaders of the colonies talked about the problems they shared. They knew the people wanted things to change, even if it meant fighting for those changes.

King George ruled England. He also ruled the American colonies.

The famous Battle of Lexington took place in the year 1775. The American colonists fought against King George's soldiers.

By 1775, fighting broke out between the king's soldiers and the American colonists. The king's troops had better weapons and more training, but the colonists were fighting for their freedom. They also knew their land well.

The Continental Congress met again in May 1775. This time the leaders of the colonies talked about their goals and their hopes. They argued about what was best for the colonies.

At last, they decided to break away from England's rule. The colonies would become a new, independent nation. That new nation would be known as the United States of America.

Thomas Jefferson, a leader from the Virginia colony, was at the Second Continental Congress. The other leaders asked him to write down their ideas. Jefferson knew what the colonists were thinking and feeling. Now he had to write it all down. This was not easy work. Those words would become the plan for a new nation, and those words would make history.

Jefferson worked on the statement from June 11 to June 28. Then he showed it to the

Thomas Jefferson wrote the document that is known as the Declaration of Independence in 1776. His work helped the American colonists to gain their freedom.

Today, the cracked Liberty Bell can be found in Philadelphia, Pennsylvania.

other leaders at the Second Continental Congress. They called the statement the Declaration of Independence. The leaders finally agreed on its exact wording on July 4, 1776. This is why July 4, the birthday of the United States, is also called Independence Day.

In Philadelphia, Pennsylvania, people gathered in the streets. They heard the Declaration of Independence read. They cheered and hugged each other as bells rang and bands played.

Colonists in other places celebrated, too. There were parades, and cannons and muskets were fired. There were speeches and special dinners. People celebrated their new nation.

In New York, the colonists were very busy. They tore down a statue of King George III. But they did not want to waste any of the metal

This man rings the Liberty Bell in 1776 to let everyone know that the Declaration of Independence had been approved.

The soldiers in the painting were called minutemen. These men wanted to help the American colonies in their fight against England. They were known as minutemen because they were ready to fight "at a minute's notice."

from the statue. They needed bullets to fight the British soldiers. So, they used the metal from the statue to make the bullets.

The colonists needed many bullets. Their struggle for freedom was far from over. They fought King George and his soldiers for seven more years in what is known as the Revolutionary War, or the American Revolution. In 1783, they finally won the war. Now they were no longer colonists. Instead, they were free citizens of the United States of America.

These two girls are wearing hats with red, white, and blue stripes. Many people wear red, white, and blue to celebrate the Fourth of July.

CHAPTER 3

Fireworks, Parades, and Food

Independence Day celebrations are special. They are often noisy, colorful, and fun. There are lots of different ways to enjoy July 4, some dating back to the time of the American colonists. We cannot think of Independence Day without thinking of the different ways to celebrate.

FIREWORKS
Lighting Up the Skies on the Fourth of July

There have always been fireworks on July 4, but they were not always the same as the ones we have today. Early fireworks were simple. The

An early Fourth of July celebration is shown here.

best ones were seen near harbors. Military ships fired off rockets over the water.

The rockets lit up the sky, but they cost a lot of money. The colonists were still fighting King George, and they did not have extra money. So they brightened the holiday by putting candles in every window.

Today, fireworks are loud and showy. The sounds they make remind us of the colonists firing cannons. There are many different kinds of fireworks. Some look like sparkling pinwheels, while others look like streamers. Still others seem like a shower of stars. Fireworks come in just about every color, including purple, orange, yellow, red, blue, and green.

Some fireworks displays are shown on the ground. Often these are shaped like objects or animals. One favorite is a sparkling red, white, and blue American flag. Another is the American eagle. Both of these things are symbols of the United States. A symbol is something that stands for something else. So, when people see American eagles and American flags, they think of the United States.

There are also other ways to light up

The colors of the American flag—red, white, and blue.

Parades are an important part of Independence Day.

Independence Day. Some larger cities have skyline celebrations. The tops of the tallest buildings stay lit all night. The Empire State Building in New York City is lit with red, white, and blue bulbs. The result is an all-American skyline.

PARADES
An Important Part of Independence Day

Parades are an important part of Independence Day. In colonial times, soldiers marched. As time passed, things changed. Fire trucks and police departments also became part of the parade. As the shiny fire engines rolled down the streets, all of the latest equipment was shown off.

Independence Day parades have grown larger than they used to be. Soldiers from America's past wars often march. Groups of scouts also may take part, along with high school bands that play marching tunes.

Many parades have floats. A float is a sort of small stage on wheels. It is pulled by a car or truck and is decorated. Some floats are of patriotic scenes. The people on them may dress in costumes, and many of the floats are in our nation's colors.

In some towns, Boy Scouts and Girl Scouts march in parades. The marchers may toss pieces of candy into the crowds of people watching. Community groups and elected officials, such as the mayor, smile and wave to everyone.

Children ride their bikes in some parades. They decorate the wheels and handlebars with colorful streamers. There may also be roller skaters in the parade. Sometimes the bikers

This woman painted her face with colors of the American flag to celebrate the Fourth of July.

and skaters wear red, white, and blue safety helmets.

The people watching the parade are also part of the fun. People line the streets, wave small American flags, and cheer for the marchers. Everyone watching wants to get a good spot. Some people come early, and many bring their own lawn chairs.

Washington, D.C., our nation's capital, has an especially large parade. Sometimes over

This Fourth of July celebration took place in Philadelphia in the year 1819.

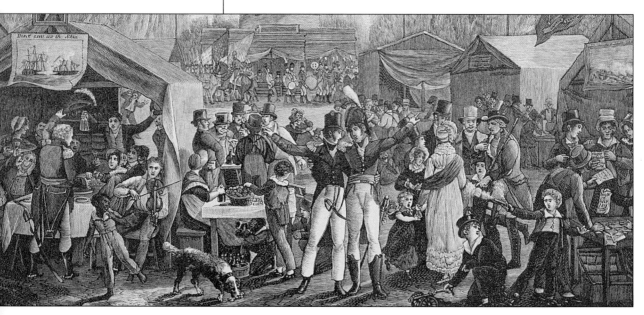

Parades have always been a fun part of Independence Day. A marching band stands on the side of the road as an old fire truck passes by.

four hundred thousand people come to see it. Bands from all over the country take part.

The Independence Day parade in Aptos, California, is unusual. It is the world's shortest parade because it is only three blocks long. However, it takes over two hours to see because it has so many marchers and floats.

The parade in Aptos is usually silly. One year, about fifty of the marchers wore pig noses and carried signs that said, "Give Me Liberty or Give Me Lard." (Lard is a kind of fat from a pig.) Aptos is a fairly small town. Some say that about half the people in town march in the parade. The rest of the people watch.

Postcards from the 1800s celebrate the Fourth of July.

FOOD
Yummy Treats on the Fourth of July

Food has always been an important part of

celebrating Independence Day. The day probably would not be as much fun without the food. In colonial times special dinners were served. The best dishes and silverware were used.

By the 1800s, things began to change. Independence Day celebrations were more relaxed. Sometimes people who were running for an elected office had big feasts. This was a good way to meet the voters.

Picnics also became popular. Families packed their picket baskets and headed to parks. Lots of other families were also there, and there were volleyball and baseball games. People also liked to pitch horseshoes, and there was music. If the park had a lake, people might swim. Sometimes they went rowing in boats.

Food is an important part of celebrating on the Fourth of July. Picnics and barbecues are popular.

One of the largest Fourth of July picnics was in Ontario, California, in 1956. It was known as the All-States Picnic, and people came from all over America. Over one hundred thousand people were there.

Americans still enjoy picnics on the Fourth of July. Many people barbecue hot dogs and hamburgers. They may also have baked beans, potato salad, and corn on the cob. These foods are all Fourth of July favorites.

Not everyone goes to a park to celebrate. Often friends and family get together in their backyards. People in cities might barbecue on their balconies and terraces.

There are some very tasty Independence Day desserts, too. Some people like a cool slice of watermelon. Others might prefer a red, white, and blue treat. Children often like to cool off with frozen desserts. On Independence Day, the red, white, and blue striped ones seem to taste best.

This building in Philadelphia was the site of the one-hundredth birthday of the United States.

CHAPTER 4

The Country's Biggest Birthdays

Independence Day is always fun-filled. Two Independence Days, however, are famous. One was our country's centennial or one-hundredth birthday. It took place in 1876. The biggest celebration was in Philadelphia, Pennsylvania. The city had a huge fair called the International Exposition. People from many countries from all over the world came to help Americans celebrate.

That Independence Day, Americans also had another special event. The public was shown a new painting of a battlefield scene from the American Revolution. The artist was Archibald

Our country's two-hundredth birthday was a lot of fun.

Willard, an American from Bedford, Ohio. Willard named the painting *The Spirit of '76*. The *'76* stands for the year 1776, when America declared its independence from England. The painting hung in Memorial Hall in Philadelphia, Pennsylvania. Many people felt it showed the courage of our soldiers. Today the painting is famous. It hangs in Abbot Hall in Marblehead, Massachusetts.

Our country's two-hundredth birthday was even more spectacular. This birthday was known as the bicentennial, and there were many activities. People in Boston made a giant Independence Day pancake that measured seventy-six inches—more than six feet—across. They also baked a huge cake that weighed sixty-nine thousand pounds. In Sheboygan, Wisconsin, people celebrated by

All of these people gathered in Philadelphia to celebrate the one-hundredth birthday of the United States.

These fire boats from New York City spray colored water in front of the Statue of Liberty.

participating in sports and games. They tossed 1,776 Frisbees™ into the air.

Washington, D.C., had the country's largest fireworks display. It cost nearly a quarter of a million dollars. New York City hosted "Operation Sail." Many tall ships sailed into

New York harbor. Over two hundred smaller ships did the same thing. Thousands of people came to watch. There were also many other celebrations throughout the United States. By the end of the day, it was clear that the United States had had a wonderful two-hundredth birthday.

The Tall Ships sailed into New York harbor to help celebrate the two-hundredth birthday of our country.

Firewords explode over the Lincoln Memorial and the Capitol Building in Washington, D.C.

CHAPTER 5

Many Ways to Celebrate

For some people, Independence Day is extra special. On this day, some people go up in hot-air balloons.

Americans like to have a good time. They are always thinking of new and exciting ways to celebrate. This is especially true on Independence Day. Some towns have holiday concerts, while others have talent shows. There are also beauty contests.

Many places put on patriotic skits or shows. Battle scenes from the Revolutionary War may be acted out. Children can enjoy pony rides, and families may go up in hot-air balloons.

Minturn, Colorado, has an all-day block party. There are pie- and hot-dog-eating contests. Everyone also enjoys the dog show and

Fireworks explode over the Lincoln Memorial (front). In the background the Washington Monunment can be seen.

the carnival. There is also plenty of food for everyone.

Philadelphia, Pennsylvania, always has great Fourth of July celebrations. After all, the Declaration of Independence was signed there. The last Independence Day in the twentieth century was on July 4, 1999. It was remembered in Philadelphia in a special way. The "Photo of the Century" was taken in front of Independence Hall. The photograph shows one hundred Americans of all different ages who were born on July 4. Each person was born in a different year from 1900 to 1999. People from all fifty states were in the photo.

The Independence Day celebration in Seward, Nebraska, is unusual. The sheriff starts the fun on July 3. He stops a car that is traveling along Interstate 80, but it is not just any car. He always picks a car with out-of-state license plates that has a family inside.

The sheriff does not arrest these people. Instead, he gives them a chance to have a great Fourth of July. The family is invited to spend

These people were all born on the Fourth of July in different years. This "Photo of the Century" was taken in Philadelphia, Pennsylvania, in front of Independence Hall on July 4, 1999.

the night at a local motel, free of charge. The next day they celebrate Independence Day with the town. The guest family can march in the parade and enjoy a pancake breakfast.

People in the town of George in the state of Washington celebrate in a big way. They make a huge cherry pie that is eight feet wide and eleven feet high. It is made with half a ton of fruit, and pieces of the pie are given out free of charge. Afterward, there is another show when the fire department hoses down the empty pie pan.

Imagine what it would be like to celebrate the Fourth of July with the United States Marines. This is exactly what some people in Albany, Georgia, have done since 1994. The public is invited to attend a celebration hosted by the United States

Fireworks light up the night sky in Washington, D.C. The Washington Monument can be seen below.

Marine Corps. There are country music concerts, carnival rides, fireworks, and much more. The idea behind the day is simple. The Marines believe we should "celebrate Independence Day with those who keep you independent."

Independence Day in Prescott, Arizona, has a western theme. The town has a weekend celebration called Frontier Days. The event

Carnival rides are a fun way to celebrate Independence Day.

Fireworks explode over the skyline of New York City.

includes a rodeo, bronco riders, and cowboys who come from near and far to compete and watch the events.

The Fourth of July can also be fun for people who live near lakes and rivers. Many people like to spend the holiday on or near the water. This is exactly what happens every Independence Day on Lake Mohawk in New Jersey. People swim and water ski during the day. When it gets dark, they can watch the fireworks from their boats.

Americans may celebrate Independence Day in different ways, but they are all celebrating the same thing. Every year, on July 4, we honor the birth of our nation. Our country stands for freedom, and there can never be too many ways to celebrate that.

Every year, on the Fourth of July, Americans honor the birth of our nation, and the people who fought to gain our country's freedom.

Independence Day Projects

★

Holiday crafts and cool cooking can make Independence Day even more special. Here are two fun things to make.

Glitter Sparkler

Make a safe sparkler to bring to a parade and wave around. You will need:

✔ **twelve 1-inch-wide strips of ribbon—four red, four white, four blue**

✔ **newspaper**

✔ **white glue**

✔ **glitter**

✔ **a blue marker or crayon**

✔ **the cardboard tube from an empty roll of toilet paper.**

✔ **a small box of stick-on stars (silver ones look best, but any color will do)**

1. Separate the ribbon strips by color and lay them flat on newspaper. Glue glitter onto one side of each ribbon.

2. When the glue is dry and the glitter is sticking, turn each ribbon over and glue glitter on the other side. Let the glue dry.

3. With the blue marker or crayon, color the cardboard tube.

4. Decorate the tube with stick-on stars.

5. Apply glue to one end of each ribbon. Glue the ends of the ribbons to the inside of the cardboard tube. Let the glue dry. Your sparkler is now done!

Celebration Ice-Cream Sundae

Red, white, and blue desserts are perfect for an Independence Day celebration. You will need:

✔ **a plastic knife***

✔ **strawberries**

✔ **a red or blue plastic dish for the ice cream**

✔ **a spoon**

✔ **vanilla ice cream**

✔ **mini marshmallows**

✔ **blueberries**

✔ **red- and blue-covered chocolate pieces**

✔ **a maraschino cherry**

1. With the help of an adult, carefully cut the strawberries in half with the plastic knife.

2. Place the strawberry halves in the plastic dish, standing them on their sides.

3. Use the spoon to place one scoop of vanilla ice cream in the center of the dish.

4. Sprinkle mini marshmallows over the ice cream.

5. Sprinkle blueberries and colored pieces of chocolate over the ice cream.

6. Put the cherry on top. Enjoy your cool Fourth of July treat!

*Safety Note: Never use a sharp knife without the help of an adult.

Words to Know

★

celebrate—To have a good time.

celebration—A party where everyone has a good time.

century—One hundred years.

colonist—A person who lives in a colony.

colony—A settlement. There were thirteen English colonies before the United States became a nation.

display—To show something.

exposition—A large fair or event attended by many people.

feast—A meal with lots of good food.

float—A small stage on wheels. Cars or trucks in parades pull floats.

historic—Having to do with the past.

Words to Know

★

lard—The type of fat that comes from a pig.

musket—A large firearm. Muskets were used as weapons in colonial times.

patriotic—Showing love and loyal support for one's country.

skyline—The outline of buildings against the sky.

spectacular—Something that is unusually good or outstanding.

symbol—Something that stands for something else.

tax—Money from the sale of things such as molasses, sugar, stamps, or tea.

territory—A region or an area of land.

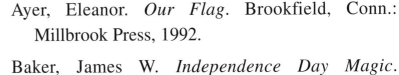

Reading About

★

Ayer, Eleanor. *Our Flag*. Brookfield, Conn.: Millbrook Press, 1992.

Baker, James W. *Independence Day Magic*. Minneapolis, Minn.: Lerner Publications, 1990.

Bingham, Caroline, and Karen Foster, eds. *Crafts for Celebration*. Brookfield, Conn.: Millbrook Press, 1993.

Cooper, Jason. *Valley Forge*. Vero Beach, Fla.: Rourke Publishing, 1999.

Craven, Jerry. *Celebrations*. Vero Beach, Fla.: Rourke Publishing, 1996.

Horg, Stan. *It's the Fourth of July!* New York: Penguin Putnam Books for Young Readers, 1995.

Kroll, Steven. *The Boston Tea Party*. New York: Holiday House, 1998.

Schleifer, Jay. *Our Declaration of Independence*. Brookfield, Conn.: Millbrook Press, 1992.

Sorensen, Lynda. *Fourth of July*. Vero Beach, Fla.: Rourke Publishing, 1994.

Internet Addresses

★

KID'S DOMAIN JULY 4TH FUN!
<http://www.kidsdomain.com/holiday/july4/
index.html>

HAPPY BIRTHDAY AMERICA
<http://www.usacitylink.com/usa/>

HAPPY 4TH OF JULY FROM ARISTOTLE—
"THE FOURTH 4 KIDS"
<http://www.aristotle.net/july4th/fourth4kids/
main.html>

Index